Through the power of poetry and prayer, the Psalms can help us connect with the present moment, cultivate gratitude and maintain a sense of well-being when dealing with life's challenges.

In this photo book, you will find a selection of Psalms especially chosen to guide your journey towards greater mindfulness and inner peace.

Also included are a series of "meditation passages" – short stories that are intended to be used as inspiration or "departure points" for moments of relaxation and reflection.

Whether you are new to meditation and prayer or have been practicing for years, this book hopes to offer a fresh perspective on the timeless wisdom of the Psalms and how they can be applied in our modern lives.

So take a deep breath, relax, and let this book guide you on your path towards greater mindfulness, gratitude and well-being.

"Light shines on the righteous and joy on the upright in heart"

Psalm 97:11

"Surely your goodness
and love will follow me
all the days of my life,

And I will dwell in the
house of the Lord
forever"

Psalm 23:6

"The Lord gives strength to his people; the Lord blesses his people with peace."

Psalm 29:11

"...the Lord blesses his people with peace."

"But you, Lord, are a
shield around me,
my glory, the One
who lifts
my head high.
I call out to the Lord,
and he answers me
from his holy
mountain"

Psalm 3:3

"...he answers me from his holy mountain."

"God is our refuge and strength, an ever-present help in trouble. Therefore we will not fear, though the earth give way and the mountains fall into the heart of the sea."

Psalm 46:1

"Therefore we will not fear..."

Nestled deep in the forest, the secluded lake was a beacon of tranquility. The pure mountain water was crystal clear and the only sound that could be heard was the harmonious swaying of the trees in the breeze.

It was here that I came to find solace from the stresses of everyday life. Whenever I felt overwhelmed or anxious, I would make my way down to the lake, where I would sit for hours, simply taking in the beauty of my surroundings.

As I sat there, watching the sunlight dance on the water, I felt all of my worries slip away. The peacefulness of the lake seemed to seep into my bones, filling me with a sense of calm and contentment.

Sometimes I would dip my toes into the cool water, feeling the silky softness of the bank beneath my feet. Other times, I would simply lie on my back, gazing up at the clear blue sky, watching the clouds drift by.

The tranquility of the secluded lake was a reminder that there was beauty and peace to be found in the world. It was a place where I could recharge my batteries and find the strength to face whatever challenges lay ahead.

"Because he loves me," says the Lord, "I will rescue him; I will protect him, for he acknowledges my name. He will call on me, and I will answer him."

Psalm 91:14

"He will call on me, and I will answer him."

"My mouth will speak
words of wisdom;
the meditation of my
heart will give you
understanding"

Psalm 49:3

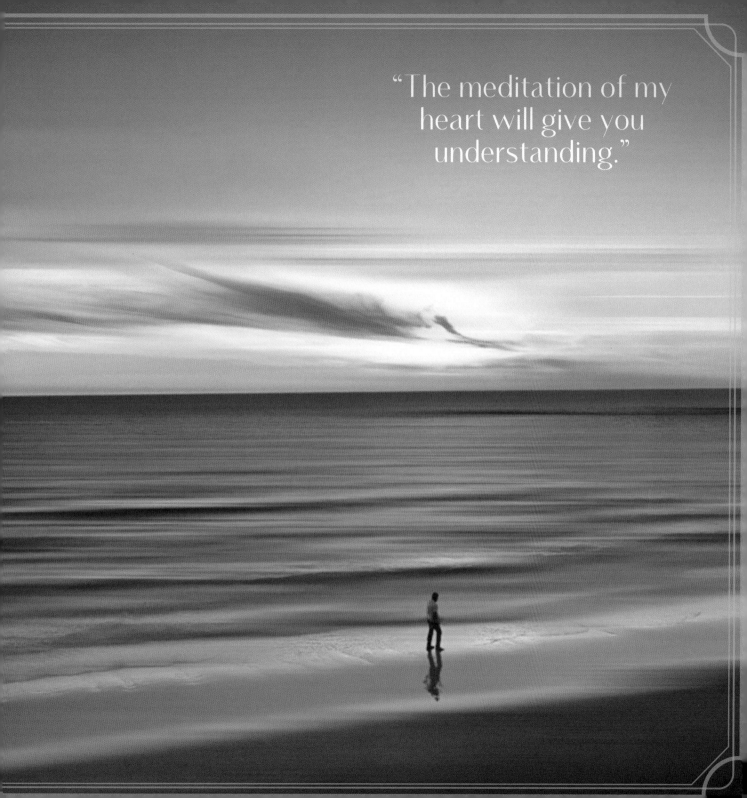

"The meditation of my heart will give you understanding."

"I sought the Lord, and
he answered me;
he delivered me
from all my fears.
Those who look to him
are radiant;
their faces are never
covered with shame"

Psalm 34:4

"Those who look to him are radiant..."

"In peace I will lie
down and sleep,
for you alone,
Lord, make me
dwell in safety."

Psalm 4:8

"For you alone, Lord, make me dwell in safety"

"That my heart may
sing your praises
and not be silent.
Lord my God,
I will praise you
forever"

Psalm 30:12

The view from the top of the mountain was breathtaking. The air was crisply fresh and the sun shone down magnificently on the world below. It was a moment of triumph, a moment to savor and celebrate.

As I sat quietly, taking in the awe-inspiring view, I felt a sense of peace and contentment wash over me. The stillness of the mountain seemed to envelop me, soothing my tired body and calming my mind.

I sat there for what felt like hours, watching the clouds roll by and the shadows shift across the beautiful landscape. And as I sat, I felt a deep sense of gratitude for the experience of climbing the mountain.

In that moment, I realized that the climb had been about more than just reaching the top. It had been about pushing myself beyond my limits, about finding my inner strength and resilience. As I sat quietly, I understood that the climb had also been about finding a connection to the earth, to the beauty and wonder of the natural world that surrounded me.

As the sun began to set and the stars came out, I knew that I would always carry that sense of peace and contentment with me, no matter where life might take me.

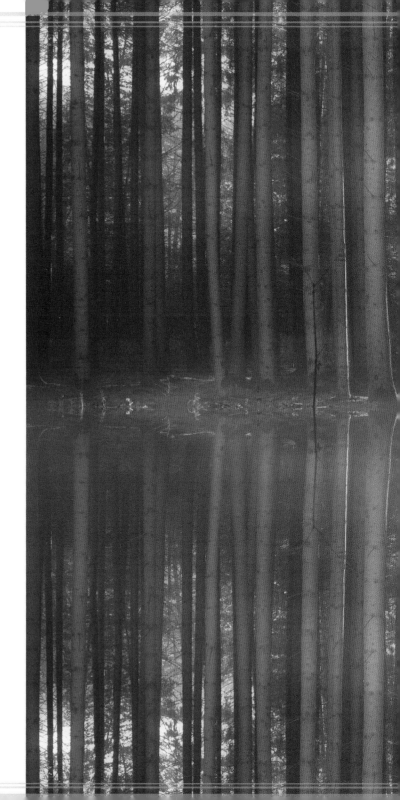

"Blessed are those
who have regard
for the weak;
the Lord
delivers them
in times
of trouble"

Psalm 41:1

"Blessed are those who have regard for the weak"

"But let all
who take refuge
in you
be glad;
let them ever
sing for joy.
Spread your
protection
over them,
that those who
love your name
may rejoice
in you"

Psalm 5:11

"...that those
who love
your name
may rejoice
in you"

"When I said,
"My foot is slipping,"
your unfailing love,
Lord, supported me.
When anxiety was
great within me,
your consolation
brought me joy."

Psalm 94:19

"...your consolation
brought me joy"

"For this God
is our God
for ever
and ever;
he will be
our guide
even to
the end"

Psalm 48:14

"...he will be our guide even to the end"

"I lift up my eyes to the mountains - where does my help come from?
My help comes from the Lord, the Maker of Heaven and earth"

Psalm 121:1

"My help comes from the Lord..."

There is nothing like coming home. I had been away for months, traveling to far-off lands and experiencing new worlds. But as much as I had enjoyed my adventures, there is nothing quite like the feeling of returning to the place where I belong.

As I stepped through the front door, I felt a wave of relief and contentment wash over me. The familiar sights and smells of home greeted me warmly, and I felt a sense of belonging that I had missed while I was away.

I wandered through the rooms, touching familiar objects and taking in the memories that they held. The comfortable sofa where I had spent endless lazy afternoons, the kitchen where I had concocted countless delights, the bookshelf filled with the stories that had shaped my life.

As I settled into my old routines, I realized that my journey had changed me in profound ways. I had seen new things, met new people, and had experiences that I would carry with me for the rest of my life.

But even as I savored the memories of my travels, I knew that there was no place like home. And as I settled into my own bed, surrounded by the familiar comforts of home, I felt a sense of peace and contentment that I had missed so much.

"Therefore my heart is glad and my tongue rejoices; my body also will rest secure, because you will not abandon me..."

Psalm 16:9

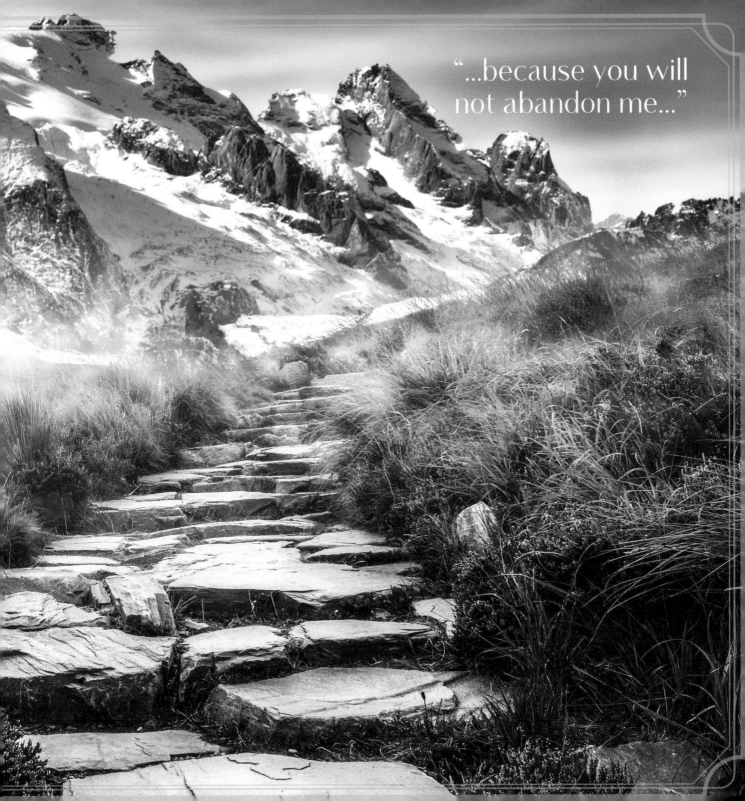

"...because you will not abandon me..."

"I keep my eyes always on the Lord.

With him at my right hand, I will not be shaken"

Psalm 16:8

"...I will not be shaken"

"The heavens declare
the glory of God;
the skies proclaim
the work of his hands.
Day after day
they pour forth speech;
night after night
they reveal knowledge"

Psalm 19:2

"The heavens declare the glory of God"

"Turn, Lord,
and
deliver me;
save me
because of your
unfailing love"

Psalm 6:4

"...because of your unfailing love"

As I sat in my favorite sun-filled spot in the park, I closed my eyes and let my mind wander. In my mind's eye, I pictured myself surrounded by loved ones, living a life filled with joy, purpose, and fulfillment.

I saw myself pursuing passions – writing, painting, travel and so many others. I saw myself in a home filled with light, laughter and those that I love most in the world.

As I continued to ruminate, I began to feel a sense of contentment and optimism. I realised while the that the path to happiness is not always easy, I would always be willing to dedicate myself to finding it.

In my mind, I saw myself overcoming challenges and obstacles with grace and resilience, and emerging stronger and more determined than ever before.

As I opened my eyes and looked around at the beauty of the park, I knew that the life I had imagined was not guaranteed. But I also knew that, with perseverance and a pinch of luck, it was entirely possible. That thought filled me with a sense of optimism and happiness that carried me through the rest of the day.

"For the Lord
is righteous,
he loves justice;
the upright
will see
his face"

Psalm 11:7

"...the upright will see his face"

"The law of the Lord
is perfect,
refreshing the soul.
The statutes
of the Lord
are trustworthy,
making wise
the simple"

Psalm 19:7

"The law of the Lord is perfect"

"The Lord is my strength
and my shield;
my heart trusts in him,
and he helps me.
My heart leaps for joy,
and with my song I
praise him"

Psalm 28:7

"My heart
leaps for joy,
and with
my song
I praise him"

"The Lord
is my shepherd,
I lack nothing.
He makes me lie down
in green pastures,
he leads me
beside quiet waters,
he refreshes my soul"

Psalm 23:1

"He refreshes my soul"

As I crossed the finish line, I felt a wave of contentment and pride wash over me. I had just completed a goal that I had been working towards for months. I took a moment to catch my breath. The sense of accomplishment that was almost overwhelming.

As I looked around at my companions, I sensed the same feelings of elation and triumph. We had all set a goal, worked hard to achieve it, and had now crossed the finish line in triumph.

The journey to this moment had been long and challenging. I had faced setbacks and obstacles along the way, but I had never lost sight of my goal. I had pushed myself further than ever before- even when it was difficult.Now, as I savored the feeling of achievement, I knew that it had all been worth it.

I hugged my family and friends who had come to support me, grateful for their encouragement and inspiration. As I looked ahead to the future, I knew that there would be other goals to set and other challenges to overcome. But for now, I was content to bask in the glow of my hard-won success.

"The precepts
of the Lord
are right,
giving joy
to the heart.
The commands
of the Lord
are radiant,
giving light
to the eyes"

Psalm 19:8

"...giving joy to the heart"

"Who may ascend
the mountain of
the Lord?
Who may stand in
his holy place?
The one who has
clean hands and a
pure heart"

Psalm 24:3

"...clean hands and a pure heart"

"He reached down
from on high and
took hold of me;
he drew me out
of deep waters"

Psalm 18:16

"...he drew me out of deep waters"

"Send me your light
and your faithful care,
let them lead me;
let them bring me to
your holy mountain"

Psalm 43:3

"Send me your light and your faithful care"

Even on the busiest of days, I find time close my eyes and take a deep breath. This moment of meditation has become a ritual that helps me find peace and balance within my busy life.

As I focus on my breath, I feel my mind begin to quiet down. The worries and distractions that had been swirling around in my head begin to fade away, replaced by a sense of calm and stillness.

I visualize a peaceful scene, imagining myself surrounded by a tranquil forest or a serene lake. In my mind's eye, I can see the colors and textures of the landscape and feel the gentle breeze on my skin.

As I continue to meditate, I feel my body relaxing and my mind becoming more clear and focused. The stresses and anxieties of the day begin to fade away, replaced by a sense of inner peace and tranquility.

When I open my eyes again, I feel a renewed sense of energy and vitality. The world around me seems brighter and more vibrant, and I feel ready to face whatever challenges lay ahead.

These moments of meditation are a daily reminder of the power of tranquility and mindfulness.

"Your love, Lord,
reaches to the heavens,
your faithfulness
to the skies.
Your righteousness is like
the highest mountains,
your justice
like the great deep"

Psalm 36:5

"Your love, Lord, reaches to the heavens"

"Keep me free
from the trap
that is set for me,
for you are my refuge.
Into your hands
I commit my spirit;
deliver me, Lord,
my faithful God"

Psalm 31:4

"Truly my soul
finds rest in God;
my salvation
comes from him.

Truly he is my rock
and my salvation;
he is my fortress,
I will never be
shaken."

Psalm 62:1

"Truly my soul finds rest in God"

"You, Lord,
keep my
lamp burning;
my God turns my
darkness into light"

Psalm 18:28

"My God turns my darkness into light"

As I walked through the cool, quiet forest, I felt my worries and anxieties begin to fade. The surrounding trees seemed to hold me in a warm embrace and the gentle sound of the leaves rustling in the breeze was like a soothing lullaby.

I had come to the forest to find peace, to escape the stresses and pressures of my busy life. I walked deeper into the woods and felt myself becoming more and more relaxed, more in tune with the rhythms of nature.

The birds and other animals seemed to sense my presence. Carefree, they went about their business with a sense of calm and ease. The sun filtered through the branches above, dappling the forest floor with golden light.

As I continued to walk, I realized that the peace I had been seeking was already within me. It was a part of me, like a hidden treasure waiting to be discovered.

In that moment, I felt a profound sense of gratitude and joy. I knew that even when I left the forest and returned to my busy life, I could carry this peace with me, like a beacon of light that would guide me through the challenges that lay ahead.

"You are radiant
with light,
more majestic
than mountains
rich with game"

Psalm 76:4

"You are
radiant
with light"

"But God will never
forget the needy;
the hope of
the afflicted will
never perish"

Psalm 9:18

"God will never forget the needy"

"The decrees of the
Lord are firm,
and all of them are
righteous.

They are more
precious than gold,
than much pure gold;
they are sweeter
than honey,
than honey from
the honeycomb"

Psalm 19:9

"They are more precious than gold"

"Even in darkness
light dawns
for the upright,
for those who
are gracious
and compassionate
and righteous"

Psalm 112:4

"...light dawns
for the upright"

Floating peacefully on my back, I felt the warm sun on my skin and the gentle rocking of the water beneath me. The lake was so still and quiet, it was as if time had stood still.

I closed my eyes and let myself drift, feeling my body becoming one with the gentle ebb and flow of the water. I felt a sense of peace and tranquility wash over me. All the cares and worries of the world had been left behind.

The breeze was cool and refreshing, carrying with it the scent of pine and wildflowers. I heard the sweet sound of a distant bird, its joyous song echoing across the water.

I opened my eyes a little, contemplating the blue sky above me, dotted with fluffy white clouds. I felt as if I was floating in a sea of sky, suspended in time and space.

For a few moments, I forgot all about the world beyond the lake. I was simply there, in the present moment, feeling the gentle embrace of the water and the sky.

As I drifted back to shore, I knew that I could carry this sense of peace and tranquility with me, like a precious memory that would stay with me forever.

Create in me
a pure heart,
O God,
and renew a
steadfast spirit
within me"

Psalm 51:10

"Create in me
a pure heart"

"How priceless is your unfailing love, O God! People take refuge in the shadow of your wings They feast on the abundance of your house; you give them drink from your river of delights. For with you is the fountain of life; in your light we see light"

Psalm 36:7

"...in your light we see light"

"Trust in the Lord
and do good;
dwell in the land
and enjoy
safe pasture.
Take delight
in the Lord,
and he will
give you
the desires
of your heart"

Psalm 37:3

"Surely you have granted him unending blessings and made him glad with the joy of your presence"

Psalm 21:6

"...the joy of your presence"

As I took my seat in the grand concert hall, I was struck by the majesty and elegance of the space. The high ceilings and luxuriously ornate decorations inspired a sense of overwhelming awe.

But it was the sound that truly took my breath away. The orchestra had just begun to play, and the rich, full-bodied music filled the air. I could feel it vibrating through my chest, and I closed my eyes and let myself be carried away by the beautiful melody.

The music was like a story unfolding before me, each note weaving a tale of beauty and passion. It was as if the composer had poured his heart and soul into every note, creating a symphony of emotion that moved me deeply.

During those moments, all else faded away. I was lost in the beauty of the music, letting it lift me and carry me away to another world.

As the final notes rang out and the applause began, I felt a sense of gratitude and wonder. I knew that I had just experienced something truly special, something that would stay with me for a long time to come.

"Show me the wonders
of your great love,
you who save
by your right hand
those who take refuge
in you from their foes"

Psalm 17:7

"Show me the wonders of your great love"

"Even though
I walk through
the darkest valley,
I will fear no evil,
for you are with me"

Psalm 23:4

"The Lord
looks down
from heaven
on all mankind
to see
if there are any
who understand,
any who seek God"

Psalm 14:2

"The Lord looks down from heaven on all mankind"

"Let the morning
bring me word of
your unfailing love,
for I have put
my trust in you.
Show me the way
I should go,
for to you
I entrust my life"

Psalm 143:8

"...to you I entrust my life"

"From the ends
of the earth
I call to you,
I call as my heart
grows faint;
lead me
to the rock
that is higher
than I"

Psalm 61:2

"Lead me to the rock that is higher than I"

As I lay down, I felt a weight begin to lift from my shoulders. I closed my eyes and took a deep breath, feeling my body relax into soft, welcoming comfort.

My mind began to wander, memories and thoughts drifting through my consciousness like leaves on a gentle autumn breeze. I let them come and go, feeling myself becoming more and more relaxed with each passing moment.

The room was quiet and peaceful. I felt cocooned in a sense of calm and safety, as if the world beyond my room had faded away.

My breathing became harmonious with my surroundings. I felt myself drifting off to sleep, carried away on a gentle tide of peace and tranquility.

As my mind quieted, I felt a wonderous sense of contentment wash over me. I knew that I was safe and loved, and that this world would be waiting for me when I returned to it.

And with that thought, I drifted off into a deep and restful sleep, feeling grateful for the peace and tranquility that had found me at last.

Printed in Great Britain
by Amazon

38062824R00064